TROUBLER

TROUBLER

Elijah Burrell

Kelsay Books

© 2018 Elijah Burrell. All rights reserved. This material may not be reproduced in any form, published, reprinted, recorded, performed, broadcast, without the express written consent of Elijah Burrell. All such actions are strictly prohibited by law.

Cover: Photograph by Elijah Burrell, *Turntable Tire*
       Design by wetsuCREATIVE

ISBN: 978-1-947465-83-1

Kelsay Books
Aldrich Press
www.kelsaybooks.com

For Polly—
who is the sum of all my blessings.

And for Grace and Lily—
who look at me like no one else ever has.

"Is that you, O troubler...?"
—1 Kings 18:17

"If thou wouldst learn the meaning of my words, heed the warnings of mine art."
—Tiresias's Monologue, *Antigone*

Acknowledgements

Many thanks to the editors of the journals where versions of these poems first appeared:

AGNI Online: "Tonight, I Wish I Were a Dirt Dauber" and "Word Search"
Birmingham Poetry Review: "Look at These Altars"
Cider Press Review: "I'm Still Here"
The New Territory: "Rapture" and "Short Life of Trouble"
North American Review: "In My Ninth Year, Troubler Gives Notice" and "In My Fifteenth Year, Troubler Returns Before Dad Leaves Mom"
Pouch Magazine: "Dirt Dweller"
Southwest Review: "By This Pond" and "Wandering Off"
Specter Magazine: "Attention Deficit"
Sugar House Review: "Rose Mallows"
Swink Magazine: "Exhibit Placard"
The Tishman Review: "Drowning" and "Field"
Unsplendid: "Exile on Highway 69," "She Knew Someone," and "Sweet Dreams of You"

"Tonight, I Wish I Were a Dirt Dauber" also appears online in an audio version at *Boombox Parade* as part of its *Online Mixtape #1*. "Exile on Highway 69," "She Knew Someone," and "Sweet Dreams of You" appear online in audio versions at *Unsplendid*. "Field" won Readers' Favorite Poem (Issue 2.1) in *The Tishman Review*.

This book would not be possible without my terrific colleagues and students at Lincoln University. I am thankful for Bennington's Writing Seminars and all the good folks there who continue to make me feel like part of the family. I am grateful for the Sewanee Writers' Conference and how, straightaway, the mountain felt like a home away from home.

Thank you to the good folks at Aldrich Press for trusting in my work.

I'm indebted to Greg Brownderville, Major Jackson, Bret Anthony Johnston, and Dora Malech for lending the world their imaginations through art, and for sparing a few kind words in support of this book.

Special thanks to the good souls at the Luther College Writers Festival, especially to Keith Lesmeister and Nancy Barry, for their incredible encouragement. Also, to the Mid-South Book Festival and the Mid-South Book Festival Student Writers Conference for giving me the chance to read, listen, and teach. A sincere word of appreciation to the St. Louis Writers' Workshop—and specifically to its director, Angela Mitchell—for asking me to read on December 4, 2016, the two-year anniversary of my mother's passing.

Thank you to Heather Dobbins, Rachel Feingold, Christian Anton Gerard, V. Hansmann, Megan Mayhew Bergman, Marc McKee, Ashley Roach-Freiman, and Shawna Rodenberg for providing places where my work could be heard, and for their hospitality.

Much gratitude to *Words on a Wire,* especially to Tim Hernandez, Daniel Chacón, and Norma Martinez, and to all the kind folks at KTEP in El Paso, for their wonderful radio show.

Thank you to April Bernard, Sven Birkerts, Patrick Boyle, Aaron Brame, Shevaun Brannigan, Victoria Clausi, Jimmie Cumbie, April Darcy, Jamie Dickson, Heather Fester, Amy Gerstler, Jen Hinst-White, Cassi Lapp, Claire McQuerry, Sebastian Paramo, **Leslie Jill Patterson**, Bill Pierce, Ruth Polleys, Melissa Range, Jess Smith, Maura Snell, Adam Vines, and Mark Wunderlich for their friendship, brilliance, and support.

Polly, Grace, and Lily, I love you. Thank you for being mine.

And finally, thank you, Dad, for your unbroken faith, your patience, and your heart.

Tracklist

TROUBLER　　　LP 1　　　SIDE A

Tonight, I Wish I Were a Dirt Dauber	17
In My Ninth Year, Troubler Gives Notice	18
Rapture	19
Dirt Dweller	20
In My Thirteenth Year, Troubler Predicts a Few Things	21
Sinkhole	22
In My Fourteenth Year, Troubler Gives Me "The Talk"	23
Field	25
In My Fifteenth Year, Troubler Returns Before Dad Leaves Mom	26
Eyes	28
Where I First Saw the Light	29

TROUBLER　　　LP 1　　　SIDE B

She Knew Someone	33
In My Nineteenth Year, Troubler Answers Some Questions	34
Unfinished Paintings and Objects	36
Stealing from the Thief	37
In My Twenty-First Year, Troubler Appears in the Form of a Woman	38
Picking Dewberries	39
In My Twenty-Third Year, Me and Troubler in the Casino Parking Lot	40
Drowning	41
Prisoner	42
In My Twenty-Eighth Year, Troubler Takes the Form of a Turtle	43
Exhibit Placard	45
Unusual Weather	46

TROUBLER   LP 2   SIDE C

Rose Mallows	49
Short Life of Trouble	50
Just War	51
In My Thirty-Fifth Year, Troubler Comes in the Form of a Poet	52
Look at These Altars	54
Half My Life	55
XS American Heart	56
Wandering Off	57
In My Thirty-Sixth Year, Troubler Makes Known a Secret	58
The New Song	59
I Can't Help	60
Attention Deficit	61
Left Telling the Story	62

TROUBLER   LP 2   SIDE D

Sweet Dreams of You	67
That Which Is Called Death Has Now Arrived	68
They Come and Take Her	69
Last Visitation	70
Word Search	71
Dead Wax	72
Exile on Highway 69	73
What a Day of Rejoicing That Will Be	74
By This Pond	75
In My Thirty-Eighth Year, Troubler Rides Shotgun to a Reading in Evansville, Indiana	76
I'm Still Here	77
Reverberations	78

Notes
About the Author

Joanne Marie Burrell
March 1955–December 2014

TROUBLER   LP 1   SIDE A

Tonight, I Wish I Were a Dirt Dauber

driven from my mud-chunk home
by pebbles slung from the wild
hands of boys.

The larders stocked, I'll feed
forever on orb weavers
and forget words like *prognosis*

and *treatment*. I'll be the sting,
not the stung, and Death
will hear my hum in his own worn-out ears.

In My Ninth Year, Troubler Gives Notice

He's white, visible in the air like smoke
from a conclave, and spins around my bed tonight.
I grip the stuffed monkey and dare not holler.
I tug the covers but know that I can't hide.
I give you notice, he says, from all around.
I seen the tape, he says. "What tape?" I say.
I seen it all, he says. *I give you notice.*

A telling:

Something moves toward you, from up the road.
The keel of your raft, built from Styrofoam
blocks, slick with algae, leaves a spoor
through the duckweed. The trees start to shadow
over the pond like an unhealthy voice.
The strike of something hidden underwater
buckles the surface. You stare. The engine kicks off,
the bobber melts. Somebody's got it.
Your heart, you know it now, is a rod
bent to the deep, just before it snaps.

"Troubler," I say. *I seen it all,* he says.

Rapture

Staring straight up from our trailer's roof, I tuned in
to the rigs flying by at night. Just me, the trucks,
and the blinking *VACANCY* by the road. The light lit
above her porch, the fresh-empty cans on the rail,
the flashing nothing-good-on-television
behind the afghan blanket she used as a curtain.
My mind was a Baptist's, my heart a psalmist's,
and I wanted so badly for her to know them both.

I'm raptured back to that trailer park's decay
when I hear a rumbling Jake brake, like a fool,
a foal breaking blind for the familiar. Unable
to square the two notions. The mystery of the holy
spirit. The imaginative pursuit of untouchable skin.
Through an expensive, efficient window, I see
the immense *ALL YOU CAN EAT* in neon
letters, lighting the future, distant dark.

Dirt Dweller

I catch a glimpse of grandeur
in a Folgers can full of dirt
and thrust my fingers into the damp
soil, then turn it over, till it up,
hunt nightcrawlers.
I used to call earthworms baby snakes.
It made them sound dangerous,
allowed me the guiltless thrill to lance
their clitella saddles with shining hooks.
I was never much for holding snakes,
but I loved the squirm and stick
of a lengthy worm.
I tip the can, just so—
skin glints from the dirt,
wiggles, submerges,
and I strike for it like a fish does dinner.

In My Thirteenth Year, Troubler Predicts a Few Things

He draws the harmonica from his pocket like a gun.
He looks like the men who spend the better part
of their days on the bench seat of a pickup truck
near the service station counter and the Coke
machine. His brogans tap the floor between breaths.
"Who are you?" I say. *I seen the tape,* he says.

He drops his harmonica hand to his side and stares
beyond me. I don't believe a word he says,
but somehow trust him. I lift my palms to him.
I don't read those, he says. *Now listen—and good.*

A telling:

You'll get bused all over, play old festivals,
stores, ninth street for sorority girls, Vermont
stage shows, estate sales, and farmers' lawns, the charm
of Cornelia street in a gunmetal city of lights
in three-hundred dollar boots, TV commercials
with a milk mustache—you name it, you'll play it—parlors.
Wooed by poets with magic tricks, bale hay,
dig graves in a bluff, climb hills in Arkansas,
love women you shouldn't on KOPN in Columbia
with Slick Nickel and the brilliant mandolin man.

"When am I going to meet the sorority girls?"
I say. *I give you notice,* he says in response.

Sinkhole

Engineers said they may have to demolish the small, sky-blue house, even though from the outside there appeared to be nothing wrong with the four-bedroom, concrete-wall structure.
—The Huffington Post, March 3, 2013

He smells the opening
soil, sees nothing.

He hears his name, his brother's yell.
As in sleep paralysis, he wakes
but can't move, can't call.
He feels his scream within his throat.
A shift brings dirt and dark
and nothing.

The living pass from sight,
they vanish
down alleyways, thumb rides
to new lives.
Something opens wide
inside them, and one day
they'll be gone.

In My Fourteenth Year, Troubler Gives Me "The Talk"

I fall to teenage sleep, and the pretty poster-
thin sweethearts, scotch-taped to my wall, parade

unending lifeless perfections to my cluttered room.
We got a problem, you creepin' thing, he says.

The top d-o-G spelled backward gives notice.
He steps from the corner, a beautiful plastic woman—

all pose—like a mannequin from Victoria's Secret.
I wonder if the bikini back is a thong.

The pseudo-woman's eyes don't even blink.
"Why are you pretending you're something you're not?"

I say. *I came all this way to ask you the same,*
he says. But his lips, under hallway light, don't move.

*I've got no smell, I've got no life, I'm well
behaved in this body. Don't that make a boy tick?*

I only know what my body says I need
from a woman. "I'll only listen to a woman who's real,"

I say. *That ain't true, you phony, not even close.
You know good and well. I give you notice.*

A telling:

*A river road. A flood. They watch from the tailgate.
She sits on his lap, occasionally pressing down.*

*He pretends not to notice. They smoke stolen Camels
she nabbed from her uncle's dashboard. Her tawny hair*

*pulled back, two wisps hang down her face for the arc
of her lips. Tires, barn doors, and uprooted snags
tussle against the undertow's draw. Her eyes
flash like spinner bait; her kiss hooks him:*

*surprising as blood in the sink after a quick brush.
He finally fathoms she's the same as him.*

*warm skin to skin, hearts pounding and focused,
the taste of smoke in their mouths. Flesh against flesh,
bone against bone. Somewhere inside them both,
souls swimming in nerves and the waters of new life.*

My body rises from the mattress—floats.
He says, *I seen the tape. I give you notice.*

Field

The remote field
near the back of my mind
holds weeds like tangled tongues,
a splintered oar in the dry fork,
quicksand.

Also:
        A woman like a dune buggy,
        all frame and wheels,

        a stethoscope like a jackpot,
            and a fiddle

        Jet winks above
        the Space Needle
        and Kerry Park
        spanning cities of possibility

        A chainsaw in its orange, plastic
        case strapped to the back
        of a dirt bike with Vermont plates

        A dead cardinal, one wing up
           like a horse chute ablaze

Inside this field grows an incurable disease.

In My Fifteenth Year, Troubler Returns Before Dad Leaves Mom

It comes up a storm, that morning, as I dress for school.
The sun unmelts orange-slow over the barn,
and rain pours in the light, no thunder or wind.

The Troubler parks on the edge of my unmade bed.
I seen the tape, he says as I drop the needle
down on Harrison's *All Things Must Pass,* side D.

A telling:

Your father, a honeyboy
from the Sunshine State,
is like a mailbox
with its flag up,
pointing to heaven.
Behind the closed door,
in the metal heat,
his heart lies stamped
for delivery to another
address.

I hear her yell. I listen at the door.
Troubler doesn't leave, and listens for himself.
She's found a plane ticket to California.

A telling:

Your mother gets left behind,
sobs out questions. She is unwell.
She snaps like stones beneath tires:
gone, gone, gone—

the scent when nothing is left but dust.

Then the "Get out, get out, get out," the last
of a double album I've always loved in the air.
I lie on the bedroom floor, squeeze my eyes shut.
I hear springs shift. The Troubler says, *A telling*.

Eyes

Before they walk back to the hotel,
he springs for a plate of pancakes.
She closes her eyes, prays.
He tries to believe
she is the one.
Her eyes spill across his face
like dishes just before they break.
He taps the table with his thumbs.

When the man was four, maybe five,
the sorrel mare broke the fence
and pushed its head
through the open kitchen window.
He cannot forget the close breath—
the enormous, eager blink.

The eyes drew him to his feet
and held him until they didn't.

Where I First Saw the Light

At six,
I dreamed they led my father to a place called The Skull.
I dreamed those on each side were my mother and another woman.
I won't tell which one waits for him now in paradise.
I dreamed God's face on the throne, wild with falling water.
I dreamed my father looked me in the eyes, said, *I thirst*.

TROUBLER   LP 1   SIDE B

She Knew Someone

She knew someone, but now he's gone
        like a cough in the cathedral:
        rapid racket, echo, stillness.
She knew someone, but now he's
        gnashing teeth around a broken straw
        while sipping milkshakes in hell.
She knew someone, but now
        she wonders. Maybe
        she never did.
She knew someone, but
        doubt bent her here and there
        like wind might do a pignut hickory.
She knew someone
        in body and bed—the biblical sense—
        when it made none.
She knew
        it wouldn't, shouldn't last,
        and it didn't.
She
        treasured herself up like a lake behind a dam
        before she finally broke in torrent.

In My Nineteenth Year, Troubler Answers Some Questions

I know the voice when the man in the next stall
begins to speak. *I wrote something,* he says.

A telling:

Two semis huddle together
on an off-ramp shoulder; hum, glow
in quiet rest beneath a sign that shines
MERGE NOW with the restless light
from every passing car.

"Have I lost my mind?" I ask the empty bathroom.
"I need to know, Troubler. I'm not right in the head."

I'm as real as you think I am. Think of yourself
as Ahab, or me as an unblind Tiresias.

I slap my skull. "Troubler, do you live in my head?"
He sings out, his voice echoing off the tiles,

These truths in God's word He has given,
How beautiful helven must be.

"I didn't catch it. Did you say helven or heaven?"
Maybe both, he says. *What I tell you is mostly from the tape.*

"What tape, Troubler? Does it tell my distant future?"
It only shows what it thinks I need to see.

"That thing you wrote, with the trucks. Is it from the tape?"
Nope, it's not. It's about finding a friend in this world.

I hear his toilet flush.

"But I don't hunt whales, Troubler."
Not that Ahab.

Unfinished Paintings and Objects

The gallery's ladder leads to what comes next.
My mind, sorry as bug dust, wonders why
I came here when I should have just stayed home.
My legs innately climb the wooden rungs,
I'm looking for new life, resurrection: a word.
All I see in front of me is black
canvas, suspended from the ceiling—a message
from above. *The word you need?* she asks. It is.
It's been a while since I've been so close to living.
The microscopic word near the corner is YES,
like snow spritzing my bare neck from a rooftop.

Stealing from the Thief

Please cut
the lights
so I
can drink
the moon's
backwash
from a
sunbeam
and make
its flavor
my own.

In My Twenty-First Year, Troubler Appears in the Form of a Woman

She brings the pot of coffee to the table, and sits
across from me. Our eyes lock like she's known
a thousand years what she has to tell me. I sip
my coffee, know it's Troubler when she opens her mouth.

They told me this body's my punishment, but I kinda like it.
"It's the best you've ever looked, Troubler," I tell her.
I kilt a snake by your pond, last time I came,
she tells me, *and they said that was some big crime.*

A telling:

*Silver-ridged
halos untwisted,
God pours peaches
from mason jars.
Fat, golden nectar
pools in a bowl.*

*the sun's a cracked egg
slapped in a bent
blue pan.*

I lean back, lift the cup to my lips, and take in what's been said.
You want me to top you off? She lifts the pot.
"I'm not sure I understand what you're trying to tell me, Troubler."
We're all unsure about something. I seen the tape.

"What on earth could you be unsure about?"
*I'm not convinced they should birth me back as a man.
I'm not convinced either one of us does it well.
God sets the breakfast table, and yet I'm hungry.*

Picking Dewberries

She is ripe, untrellised, a green-eyed story
brambling. She plucks a few berries, shapes
the loose fabric of her dress like a sack to gather
them, carry them home, carry me home.

When she presses the fruit into my mouth,
I spear it with my tongue, and spin
each half's seeds through the sugary juice.
The inside of her leg presses to my leg.

I've never known, until this moment,
such longing for a berry. She chews
one, takes her time. Her eyes say welcome
home—say pick your berries well.

And all I want is to be home.

In My Twenty-Third Year, Me and Troubler in the Casino Parking Lot

"You know they don't even use tapes anymore,"
I say. *I don't know what you're talking about,*

he says. "Just trying to keep you current in your troubling."
You saying I'm outmoded? That's a real hoot.

I'm current with the times—you need to know that.

I bug out my eyes—try to sound like a kook,
"I kind of feel a telling coming on,

Troubler." *A broken videocassette forsaken in the street:
iridescent entrails tickle the curb
awhile.*

He watches the sign's bright bulbs chase one another
in relentless strobe, then his eyes slowly widen.

*Waitadadblameminute. Am I the curb
or the entrails?* "You've seen the tape. Why don't you tell me?"

Drowning

You have no idea
because, through your lens, this
doesn't look like drowning.

> *Second grade, we soaked-shirt relayed in the pool*
> *near my school. Each pal, one after the other, bound*
> *the next in a sweatshirt like a trap, or a net.*
> *I was last in line when the boy, whose name I've forgotten,*
> *pulled the sopping shirt over my head, and pushed*
> *me from the edge.*
> *I didn't flail.*
> *I didn't fight.*
> *I drowned*
> *in secret.*

Today I switch off my head,
mouth dangling open, eyes like muddied glass.
I turn backstroke to backslide, wine to water.
My body hollers, *Breathe.*
Oh, holy rollers, *Breathe.*
My arms and legs, groundless, run
up the fluid steps like ladder-climb.
Drowning doesn't look as you'd expect.
When caught by the skin of the water, we lock
ourselves out, appear still as we fight suffocation.

> *The adults were angry. They could not understand*
> *why a good, happy boy would just float, sink slow,*
> *not fight. "Why didn't you yell for help?" they said.*
> *"You should have yelled for help," they said and wondered.*

One must breathe before calling for help.
One must breathe before deciding to live.
Do not fear the water.
Let me show you the deep.

Prisoner

A police car pulls
up to the red light,
transfer prisoner
in back. He takes
each detail in:
empty children's
seats behind me,
chopper riding
the sky.

Our eyes pass one
another, my face
an enticing puzzle.
Beside me, the phone
buzzes, "Let's do
the movie tonight
if Mom & Dad
can babysit"—
I'm startled from
the phone by horns.
The light gone green,
the prisoner's car
has moved along.
I think to myself
how nice it'd be
to get out, see
something new.

In My Twenty-Eighth Year, Troubler Takes the Form of a Turtle

At Cunningham's pond, the head of a painted turtle
dips below the surface. I wade out,

twigs and the chill of mud between my toes.
I walk out deep enough the water splashes

my chin. I cast a line: a plastic worm,
still greasy from the pack, wiggles and drips

a trail as it flies. Back on the truck, my clothes
heaped on the hood, water dries brown and sticky

on my skin. Troubler's a turtle, by god—hard shell
and all. He lifts his head to look at me.

It came to me in hi-fi sound, my boy,
in three-head picture clarity, he says.

A telling:

One boy grabbed a hook, one grabbed his ax.
They got a big ole snapper, a mean ole thing,
fast faced and gator tailed. When they hooked her head
and yanked it from its shell like a tug of war,
brother brought down the ax and the turtle lost
its tough. Little cousin tied her up. She dripped
black-red to the last drop. The blade blazed, slit
her skin clean open. They tossed her body in the pot.
Mama cooked it all day. The boys loved her so.
Sometimes they drew their mama stars in the dust.
She filled their bowls with toes, bones, neck and all.

When he's quiet, he pulls his head back into his shell.
I remember the bottle of nail polish on the floorboard.

As I write TROUBLER across his back, I say,
"Turtler, tell me in truth: Is that some weird story

you just made up?" *In truth?* he slowly says,
I give you notice. He leaves the empty shell.

Exhibit Placard

He sits alone on a corner bench,
same spot each day. The museum teems,
even on Mondays. The corridors pump,
pump like atria. Closing his eyes, he stirs
in one-sided exchanges with his closest
  strangers.
He breathes in their company. The echoed squawk
of infants, the clack-clack-clack of heels arouse
his ears. The voices of fathers, husbands vibrate
within his sapless body.

Unusual Weather

I never look for you,
        unusual weather. You rain
mirrors in which my face
        reflects fact, reels in
my eyes too late. Speed trap
        in the median, chest of stolen
goods, you offer change.
        I will not call you destruction,
bandage of enticement.
        Each time I see you, my heart
blooms a tar-paper skin.
        I sleep on your floor
in the doorway.
        Bone-pellet belly
of bourbon and *no*.
        Years bend like teaspoons
washed into garbage
        disposals: nicked sharp
and out of shape.

TROUBLER   LP 2   SIDE C

Rose Mallows

He guessed her tattoo was rose mallow, though suspected
that when beneath the needle, she'd requested
a hibiscus from the skin calligrapher

above her. This gave him the chance
to trace the flower's figure across her shoulder
blade, to tell her about the mallows by the pond

back home. How, as a boy, he grazed their petals
with two fingers, watched the bees work nearby.
She said, "It's a hibiscus. I love how it looks

on my back." He told her how he lay in the reeds
by the bank, cane pole beside him, chose the brightest
bunch to carry back up the path for the vase

on his mother's table. Such a coincidence
how much it favored the rose mallows, he said.
Her husband picked roses, but she was happy

she'd gone with something transparent, gauzy, rare.
Roses are a snooze, she thought. He set her wine glass
on the hotel sink, stepped into her smile.

Eyes closed, he could clearly see the mallows mowed
by his father's edger—not by the pretend pond,
the concocted bees or vase. The ditch.

Short Life of Trouble

You can't come looking for something fancy.
It's Stafford-on-Springfield, Highway 44,
not Stratford-on-Avon.
The menthol light dangles from her lips
as she recites Sonnet 103 from memory,
straddles the edge of the bed in a Motel 6.
This morning, pregnant clouds rain shadows down
across the bass boat and RV dealerships.

She knows her God is near, because where two
are gathered (she and Shakespeare), He is present.
Continental breakfast noise pours through
holes in thin sheetrock, a car alarm
from just outside the door. All this racket, shadows
spreading over the lots, heaping ashtray,
Gideon's Bible hidden in the drawer beneath
the pizza delivery menus

swallow her whole like a snake's hot jaws—forever
pulling and crushing her with holy perfection.

Just War

Raindrops pelt the Little Maumelle, nothing
like payload from a drone.
As they strike lily pads rich and green,
katydids keep perfect time
beneath the noise of the highway
bridge. Spring peepers. Gurgling streams
of melted ice. A coon eyes the wink
of an ascending jetliner.
Somewhere a girl listens to the sound
of an approaching jet fighter.

Somewhere I turn off my television,
my porch light, oblivious to it all.

In My Thirty-Fifth Year, Troubler Comes in the Form of a Poet

...And the cotton making every day, he reads
graveside, like a singing knife, outside Cotton Plant,

Arkansas. I look around. I can't
remember why I'm here. Troubler's suit is bespoke

with an anomalous purple design inside the jacket.
The Lord's pattern is paisley, he says as his wingtips

dig the delta clay. Troubler likes to whistle,
even in a graveyard, and that just gives me the creeps.

The sound is flat and dark as Peetie Wheatstraw's
headstone. "No respect for the dead?" I say.

I heard your someday-voice on the tape, he says.
I seen your words to come, he says.

"Tell me the sound, Troubler. What have you heard?"
The graves fall away, the church is gone, and we sit

in the front seat of a Ford, in designer suits,
and listen to "You Gotta Move" by the Stones,

the same song as dead Wheatstraw's "Ice and Snow
Blues" but not nearly as lived in and weary of the world.

I *did more for you than you understand.*

A telling:

*Take an endless pull from that fermented cupful
he swallowed. Be word-boozed like the pit-livered voice
of Swansea. Go stand in the Jordan, let the glaze of honey
hang on your breath. Pick your dinner of locusts from the bank
as they wash past your knees on down to the Dead Sea.
You are empty, dragged bloodless and featherless from the coop.
You chuck clods like grenades, rub your hands through the filth.
Your call hooks folks fishing by the riverside.
You're not Dylan or Dylan or Frank or Dubya-Bee.
You sparkle like ditch weed, spotted from a teen's car.
Sparkle like ditch weed, spotted from a teen's car.
You collection of various facades.
You limited-edition Americana encyclopedia
You are just a limited Elijah.*

Do you think the lapels on this jacket are too skinny? he asks.
"I am just a limited Elijah," I say.

Look at These Altars

For Jimmie

Look out that window, framed within
the perfect wall, while the whole house burns
behind us.

On the other side, the trout lilies spring, the chorus
frogs heave like thumbs rake the plastic bristles
on combs.

On the other side, it clouds over like lipstick
smears on the rim of a glass—her eyes
distant lightning.

On the other side, the brick wall of an abandoned
building says, *I followed you big river,*
in graffiti swirl.

On the other side, out past the steering wheel,
the lake spreads her arms so wide and ripples
into bright nothing.

Look out that window, framed within
the perfect wall, while the whole house burns
behind us.

Half My Life

In past lives or dreams,
I'm a bear unsuited
to recline on the ice
shelves along a cold highway,
or paw-plink the keys
of a baby grand.

I fell through you, somehow, wet
with music and breath, to get to then
and someday, with thumbs to play
and ears to know.

I am now the color of nothing,
falling through trapdoors
in the middle of night.
The door slides shut above me,
a piano beneath me, wind
in my ears for the long drop.

XS American Heart

I.

You walk like Rickenbacher clang, red race
stripes painted down your body, bronze strings and a hundred
volts rolling through your veins. When you're in a room,
every light for a thousand miles covers you, bathes
you, cleans you up, and makes you holy. Here's a cheek.
Smack it. Here's the other. Strike till it's red.
Once you're done, take my coat and leave me here for dead.
Then come back and find me on this road to Damascus.

II.

I believe the flight attendant's body
must smell and squeak of hotel soap
and water, wonder how much sleep she got
last night, notice her diamond ring,
before my head dips above and below
the waters of unsettled sleep.

III.

Your song musters me skyward
above the lustrous scrapers
and humming plains of midwest farms.
I make a descent to your redbud lips,
as inviting as airfield lights. You lie
beneath the tarmac of sheets. You wait
for me to come in for a rough landing.

IV.

Your hair, in loose configurations,
a sky of geese, climbs and dives in the air,
rallies the weakness in my XS American heart.

Wandering Off

The quarter horse strides through the switchgrass
toward my father. He slides the bit into its mouth.
Its tail sways as he sets the saddle blanket
on its back in the late sunlight.
The horse's neck bows toward him,
and he stares as if he can almost see himself
in its dark eye. My mother tells him something,
or perhaps her gentle voice is directed to the horse.
Her small hand skims its cheek
as she speaks. He crouches down
to give her a leg up, and looks to her
with incredible patience.
We watch her ride across the field and dissolve.

My eyes open on metallic wallpaper
next to the hotel-room bed. A thin sheet
of light beams from the space between the curtains
that don't quite fit together. I look down
at the floor, the graveyard
of pillows, and stare at my lone reflection
in the television screen.

In My Thirty-Sixth Year, Troubler Makes Known a Secret

Do we have a few minutes alone? I've got something to tell you, he says. *I seen the tape. You need to be ready.*

A telling:

> *The pounds slip off her belly, hips, and arms*
> *like rainwater, easy and careless.*
> *Meanwhile, something cloaked and hard grows in her.*
> *Your dad loves her new diminishment.*
> *The pounds slip off her belly, her hips, her arms,*
> *like a creek full of rainwater glides easy and careless.*
> *When you were a little boy, you rested your ear*
> *on the warm cushion of her chest.*
> *You measured your breath to match hers.*
> *You sank with the give of her heavier body,*
> *felt the beat of her heart through her yellow shirt.*
> *Your imagination rejoiced in her rhythmic foreverness.*
> *When you were a boy, you rested your ear*
> *on the warm cushion of her chest*
> *and measured your breath to match hers.*

I'm sorry I trouble you.
Then he disappears.

The New Song

Play me some old songs, she says.
I move my way from Beatles and Stones
to the American soil of Hank Williams
and Paul Simon. Some verses
she bobs her head to, before her tongue
dries, and she sips Coke from her straw.

When my own voice quiets, I hear hers.

She closes her eyes when I miss the chord
on a song I've never tried to play.
I've heard its hurt a thousand times,
slap the strings when I can't get it right.
Let's not worry about that new song,
she says.

Her skin is dim, like a faded picture
from a kept Sunday paper. *Another Elvis,*
she says.

She mouths the words, my fingers switch
from pressing four strings down to three,
the *F* to *C*. My voice, crude, cracks.
I do the best I can.
Put a chain around my neck
and lead me anywhere,
we sing.

I Can't Help

A wise voice says, *Shelter in place within
yourself, your entrails. Have guts.*
I do, but it involves my strongest parts
torn apart. I can't
      help
      failing
            in all I do.
Would you like me to stay? You say, *Sing it again.
Darling.*
      So
      you
           go.
Some things are meant to be.

You say your pain comes in short bursts of voice,
like the sound of a falling quarter through a jukebox's innards.
I see you as a decaying wooden box—
something from the past that still holds a song.
Your red and blue lights shine in the nearby mirror
tonight, throw light into your voyaging eyes.

Attention Deficit

All of us
gabble and yelp and caterwaul
even the war mutters in the gutter
between the borders
of our fame-leaning lives
no one bothers
to listen
mine is some voice blabbering
just under the pit's strings
from behind the curtains
on and on and on
come see what I've written
come see me enact it
someone
kiss my mouth
shut

Left Telling the Story

> *What prowess is it to slay the slain anew?*
> —Tiresias in *Antigone*

Your life was yours, not mine,
and I worry I'm treating you
more like a puppet, a doll,
a thing for entertainment.

I'm trying to put away the games,
treat you less delicately than God
will, or is, or has. It's not easy.
I want to give you everything.

You are not a prop, a ruse,
or something I use for effect.
And yet, when I approach you,
get up close to you, show you,

you're not alive, not alive.
Something's gone, move along,
I say to myself, but I can't
not tell how your hurt sank fangs

inside you, like a low E
hammer-on, and a pull-off,
a power chord when you spoke

or choked to *Nobody else
is here, Mom.* I wore your favorite
outfit like a costume that night
I thought you'd die, and tried

to make each word a sweet one,
every song a great one—

Lennon/McCartney, Keats, Yeats,

the converted apostle Paul.
You couldn't say, *I'm thirsty*,
so I sponged your tongue with water.
Understand, I'm not working your crossbar

side to side. I'm not clothing
you in a new white dress,
or brushing the nothing where your hair
fell fresh from your living head.

I'm no ventriloquist.
I'm not writing a final scene to rehearse again and again
just to watch your eyelids untense.

TROUBLER LP 2 SIDE D

Sweet Dreams of You

It's going to be okay. I'm right here, I promise.
End eyes below Mom mix wait country
Trail tail bucket concerned cornered dig crossing
Echo system whip crack interruption talk beat shrug
I fish am worm sorry kiss I lured made them
Feel me how dares from speaking above try high
Only she knows pain pump people fooling muscles sweet
It's going to be ok the sonnet can't die.

Gone clothes winter short triangle face anything
From ozone sage humming windows gold
Me baggage men watch door pieces fifteen clean off
Stew say stay tramadol so stone fate face games
While I move start life plain in mud ring clear
The night sweet you, dreams you of someone gone.

That Which Is Called Death Has Now Arrived

That spell between *We have to talk about something,
son* and this moment, was white noise of questions,
yellow jackets' repeated stings, an ice-house
mind: myeloma, time disrupter.

      Spirit,
Inhale the salt breath of whatever sea you've found.
Please, wake up, wonder, *What has happened to me?*

They Come and Take Her

The funeral man and his wife park out front,
knock on the door. They knew her and are very sorry,
so sorry, for our loss. "Take a few minutes,"
they say. I'm alone. I speak to an empty figure
in a room that saw the deaths of her mother and father,
a room that saw her finally give in and go.
I watch the violent shaking of the stretcher, of her body,
as they roll her from room to porch to hearse.
The makeshift bed bangs, slides into the blind
rear quarters. Vanishing act. The funeral man
stands beside me. "She's in a better place,"
he says. "It was tough, there, in the end," he says.
"The Lord has a plan," he says, and I weakly nod.
"Hot damn, it's cold out here," he says. "It's cold."

Last Visitation

I stepped forward and the floor chasmed like the Sea
of Galilee. She lay in a dark room for a day.
Then the funeral man rolled her to the far end
of the very large room beneath fluorescent lights.

When she was alive, she'd never needed lights.
I was her fireworks show, a cherry bomb
in a mailbox, the whistler through her smoky sky,
a string of ladyfingers on the dock by our pond,
the Black Cats, the Roman candle held in her hand.

Another step, and my legs wobbled
across the unpredictable space. I walked
that uncertain floor, one foot over the next—
no sounds, no songs. My body atremble, hers a shell
sunk in the dark water of a lake.

When I felt her stubble of hair on my cheek—her lips,
dried, against mine—that very last time, I knew
I could only ever be the residual light
from a sparkler, after its stick has moved through empty space.

Word Search

Donkey was the only one she'd found
in the puzzle called "Pets." The circle, wavy
across the left side. The word struck
through with a confident lead line.

She never found *Cat* curled near the top,
or unchameleoned *Lizard* dead
center, backward *Guinea Pig* hid.
Hard to find energy to chase *Canary*.

I wonder if she closed her eyes
against the book. I see, now,
the book's next puzzle is "In the Air"—
devoid of marks.

Unfound *Aroma*, *Drizzle*, and *Dust*.
I think of *Wind*, and what it does
to a cotton dress. How, in a *Haze*,
her voice made me so glad and hopeless.

The *Butterfly*, so light and whole
and clear, quickly taken from the air.

Dead Wax

Last night, I finally learned what you meant to me
when you were always not gone away. I'll watch
the sun today. Watch the pick-a-color sky
haul the bright balloon in its mouth. Drag it dazzling hot
and west. In my newest chronic dream, there's nothing
but your ever-open eyes. I force mine shut.
They're damp, as yours were not. I see your eyes
unshut. Some people see faces in a cloud,
some in the way a slice of toast toasts strangely.
If this were a song, you'd hear the harmonies here.
But I can't sing, today, and you can't listen,
so let's let the hissing dead wax carry us out.

Exile on Highway 69

I hear her talking when I'm on the road.
On the long haul to Dallas, handfuls of sleet
buckshot the windshield, a kamikaze cadence
of BBs on glass. *Death* is the final word,
but still she talks to me over winter weather,
over the sound of every other voice.
The ice pellets ricochet off the car,
detonate in the air like confetti announces
finale. What a beautiful buzz. What a buzz.
I push past the hulking bodies of mammoths—
cars ditched and buried in snow listening for rescue.
The minutes grow. The light moons from above.
I haven't heard from you in over a year,
Troubler. You're going to be the death of me.

What a Day of Rejoicing That Will Be

Take me to the arms
of my mother,
O channel cat, O hogsucker.

Float my body on the surface
when it's finally time to see her.
Lift this swollen frame
as if it were a bulrush ark.

Healers, piece it together
in your house of life.
Pull the shoes from its feet,

uncover its face.
Cleanse it from what it's done and seen.
Stretch out your hands,
reveal your wonders.

By This Pond

By this pond, where I slowly adapt to me without,
where I gradually get the fact I'm half a shape,
where I remember what it's like to crave,

and where I cast a line and watch it fall
closer each time to its imagined target,
delighting in the gear-spin of the handle.

This speed will catch the fish's eye, this speed
impersonates the thing the fish wants most.

I brought my friend to this pond, and he said it was hell
waiting for a fish to bite. I told him
the heaven is in that hell. He didn't get it.

A jolt, and my rod bends to the deep, its tip
almost submerged. In the air one half stretches
to meet its rough reflection on the water.
This shape, I know it now. Only in being
bent, does the heart become the heart it's meant to.

In My Thirty-Eighth Year, Troubler Rides Shotgun to a Reading in Evansville, Indiana

If I crash right now and die waiting for a cop
or passerby, trapped in a ditch full of smoke
and glass, the plastic dash smashed against my chest,
I would not want to serenade the responders
descending the embankment, the rubberneckers falling
into formation to hear my stereo speakers
blaring Mike + The Mechanics' "Living Years"
to all, me staring at nothing particular.

Troubler is two feet away. It's been a year
of silence, like the tape has paused or stopped.
"Please speak," I say. He watches the trees and signs
rewind to old beginnings we'll never get back to.
I replay the night and moment, again, in my mind.

Dad balanced his unplugged Strat by her bed, that night,
to fetch us coffee after strumming The Beatles'
"She's a Woman." Minutes later, the moment
came as she slipped out through the eye of a needle.

In the grand scheme, that song's not mediocre.
"Grand scheme" sounds underhanded. I know the score,
Lord—who died for whom. The song that played
her out, from my father's fingers, was one I can live with.

I flinch as a goldfinch flashes across the windshield.
The yellow streak a reminder of the speed things change.
"I've got to bow out of this death march, Troubler," I say,
but he's gone too. His voice is in my ear:
When I get back, this life better be picked up.

I'm Still Here

For Dad

Tell everybody I'm still kicking and stomping,
just not quite as high.
Didn't have much for lunch, had an avocado
for breakfast. Ran a rag over the counter,
nudged the broom across the bedroom floor.
Feet don't move how they did.
Watched the ceiling
from her side of the bed.
Washed the pillowcase
from her side of the bed.

Unfolded a lawn chair beside the chicken pen.
The hens pecked at the snow a bit then disappeared
into their coop.

Woke up this morning,
found one of her combs
behind the toaster.
Not a bit of hair between the bristles.

Reverberations

One day, I heard the neighbor boys make war.
I recognized the sounds. One yelled, *I got you—you're dead.*
The other shrieked from the ghost bullet, chest blown open.

That's not how it sounds when someone dies, the first boy yelled.
Once I called her number and let it ring for the voicemail,
but reached a number that had been disconnected or was

no longer in service. There are so many ways to hear it.
A robin flies away from its nest, disappears
into sunlight. That quiet. Today, it's exactly that quiet.

But last night I sat on the back porch and listened
to the newborn calf bellow from its hutch
across the pasture. From the far darkness, its mother
called out. From the far darkness, its mother.

Notes

Troubler's telling near the end of "In My Thirteenth Year, Troubler Makes a Few Predictions" was inspired by a letter Harmonica Frank Floyd once wrote to music critic Greg Shaw.

Troubler's telling in "In My Fourteenth Year, Troubler Gives Me 'The Talk'" envisions the Great Flood of 1993, along the Missouri and Mississippi rivers and their tributaries.

"In My Nineteenth Year, Troubler Answers Some Questions" contains a conversation between Troubler and the poem's speaker concerning individuals and characters from 1 Kings 18:17 in the King James Bible, Sophocles's *Oedipus Rex* and *Antigone*, T.S. Eliot's *The Waste Land*, and Herman Melville's *Moby-Dick*.

"Unfinished Paintings and Objects" was inspired by the title of Yoko Ono's 1966 art exhibition at the Indica Gallery, in London, where she met John Lennon.

"Short Life of Trouble" takes its title from a quote in *True Dylan*, the famous 1987 *Esquire* interview/one-act play written by Sam Shepard about Bob Dylan.

"The New Song" and "I Can't Help" allude to the lyrics of Elvis Presley's songs "I Can't Help Falling in Love" (written by Hugo Peretti, Luigi Creatore, and George David Weiss) and "(Let Me Be Your) Teddy Bear" (written by Kal Mann and Bernie Lowe).

"Exile On Highway 69" alludes to lyrics from three songs on The Rolling Stones' 1972 *Exile on Main Street*. The first line contains a variation on the initial line from "Rocks Off," the album's first song. The ninth line includes a few words from the middle of "Loving Cup," the ninth song. The fourteenth line of the poem incorporates bits of the last line of the album's last song, "Soul Survivor."

"That Which Is Called Death Has Now Arrived" takes its title from a line in *The Tibetan Book of the Dead*.

About the Author

Aldrich Press published Elijah Burrell's first poetry collection, *The Skin of the River*, in 2014. He received the 2010 Jane Kenyon Scholarship at Bennington College, where he earned his MFA in Writing and Literature at Bennington's Writing Seminars. In 2012 Burrell joined the faculty of Lincoln University in Jefferson City, Missouri. An assistant professor in Lincoln's Department of Humanities and Communication, Burrell teaches creative writing and literature. He resides near Jefferson City, Missouri.

www.ingramcontent.com/pod-product-compliance
Lightning Source LLC
LaVergne TN
LVHW040743250326
834688LV00031B/420